DATE_____

I AM GRATEFUL FOR…

1. _____
2. _____
3. _____

WHAT WOULD MAKE TODAY GREAT ?

1. _____
2. _____
3. _____

DAILY AFFIRMATIONS. I AM…

1. _____
2. _____
3. _____

BEST PART OF MY DAY TODAY

_____
_____
_____

HOW COULD I HAVE MADE TODAY BETTER?

_____
_____
_____

Date_____

I AM GRATEFUL FOR...

1. _____
2. _____
3. _____

WHAT WOULD MAKE TODAY GREAT ?

1. _____
2. _____
3. _____

DAILY AFFIRMATIONS. I AM...

1. _____
2. _____
3. _____

BEST PART OF MY DAY TODAY

_____
_____
_____

HOW COULD I HAVE MADE TODAY BETTER?

_____
_____
_____

Date_____

I am grateful for...

1. _____
2. _____
3. _____

What would make today great?

1. _____
2. _____
3. _____

Daily Affirmations. I am...

1. _____
2. _____
3. _____

Best part of my day today

_____
_____
_____

How could I have made today better?

_____
_____
_____

Date_____

I am grateful for...

1. _____
2. _____
3. _____

What would make today great?

1. _____
2. _____
3. _____

Daily Affirmations. I am...

1. _____
2. _____
3. _____

Best part of my day today

_____
_____
_____

How could I have made today better?

_____
_____
_____

Date_____

I AM GRATEFUL FOR...

1. _____
2. _____
3. _____

WHAT WOULD MAKE TODAY GREAT ?

1. _____
2. _____
3. _____

DAILY AFFIRMATIONS. I AM...

1. _____
2. _____
3. _____

BEST PART OF MY DAY TODAY

_____
_____
_____

HOW COULD I HAVE MADE TODAY BETTER?

_____
_____
_____

Date_____

I am grateful for...

1. _____
2. _____
3. _____

What would make today great ?

1. _____
2. _____
3. _____

Daily Affirmations. I am...

1. _____
2. _____
3. _____

Best part of my day today

_____
_____
_____

How could I have made today better?

_____
_____
_____

Date_____

I am grateful for...

1. _____
2. _____
3. _____

What would make today great?

1. _____
2. _____
3. _____

Daily Affirmations. I am...

1. _____
2. _____
3. _____

Best part of my day today

_____
_____
_____

How could I have made today better?

_____
_____
_____

Date_____

I AM GRATEFUL FOR...

1. _____
2. _____
3. _____

WHAT WOULD MAKE TODAY GREAT ?

1. _____
2. _____
3. _____

DAILY AFFIRMATIONS. I AM...

1. _____
2. _____
3. _____

BEST PART OF MY DAY TODAY

_____
_____
_____

HOW COULD I HAVE MADE TODAY BETTER?

_____
_____
_____

Date_____

I AM GRATEFUL FOR…

1. _____
2. _____
3. _____

WHAT WOULD MAKE TODAY GREAT ?

1. _____
2. _____
3. _____

DAILY AFFIRMATIONS. I AM…

1. _____
2. _____
3. _____

BEST PART OF MY DAY TODAY

_____
_____
_____

HOW COULD I HAVE MADE TODAY BETTER?

_____
_____
_____

Date_____

I am grateful for...

1. _____
2. _____
3. _____

What would make today great?

1. _____
2. _____
3. _____

Daily Affirmations. I am...

1. _____
2. _____
3. _____

Best part of my day today

_____
_____
_____

How could I have made today better?

_____
_____
_____

Date_____

I AM GRATEFUL FOR...

1. _____
2. _____
3. _____

WHAT WOULD MAKE TODAY GREAT ?

1. _____
2. _____
3. _____

DAILY AFFIRMATIONS. I AM...

1. _____
2. _____
3. _____

BEST PART OF MY DAY TODAY

_____
_____
_____

HOW COULD I HAVE MADE TODAY BETTER?

_____
_____
_____

DATE_____

I AM GRATEFUL FOR...

1. _____
2. _____
3. _____

WHAT WOULD MAKE TODAY GREAT?

1. _____
2. _____
3. _____

DAILY AFFIRMATIONS. I AM...

1. _____
2. _____
3. _____

BEST PART OF MY DAY TODAY

_____
_____
_____

HOW COULD I HAVE MADE TODAY BETTER?

_____
_____
_____

Date_____

I am grateful for...

1. _____
2. _____
3. _____

What would make today great?

1. _____
2. _____
3. _____

Daily Affirmations. I am...

1. _____
2. _____
3. _____

Best part of my day today

_____
_____
_____

How could I have made today better?

_____
_____
_____

Date_____

I am grateful for...

1. _____
2. _____
3. _____

What would make today great?

1. _____
2. _____
3. _____

Daily Affirmations. I am...

1. _____
2. _____
3. _____

Best part of my day today

_____
_____
_____

How could I have made today better?

_____
_____
_____

Date_____

I am grateful for...

1. _____
2. _____
3. _____

What would make today great?

1. _____
2. _____
3. _____

Daily Affirmations. I am...

1. _____
2. _____
3. _____

Best part of my day today

_____
_____
_____

How could I have made today better?

_____
_____
_____

Date_____

I am grateful for...

1. _____
2. _____
3. _____

What would make today great?

1. _____
2. _____
3. _____

Daily Affirmations. I am...

1. _____
2. _____
3. _____

Best part of my day today

_____
_____
_____

How could I have made today better?

_____
_____
_____

DATE_____

I AM GRATEFUL FOR...

1. _____
2. _____
3. _____

WHAT WOULD MAKE TODAY GREAT?

1. _____
2. _____
3. _____

DAILY AFFIRMATIONS. I AM...

1. _____
2. _____
3. _____

BEST PART OF MY DAY TODAY

_____
_____
_____

HOW COULD I HAVE MADE TODAY BETTER?

_____
_____
_____

Date_____

I am grateful for...

1. _____
2. _____
3. _____

What would make today great?

1. _____
2. _____
3. _____

Daily Affirmations. I am...

1. _____
2. _____
3. _____

Best part of my day today

_____
_____
_____

How could I have made today better?

_____
_____
_____

Date_____

I AM GRATEFUL FOR...

1. _____
2. _____
3. _____

WHAT WOULD MAKE TODAY GREAT ?

1. _____
2. _____
3. _____

DAILY AFFIRMATIONS. I AM...

1. _____
2. _____
3. _____

BEST PART OF MY DAY TODAY

_____
_____
_____

HOW COULD I HAVE MADE TODAY BETTER?

_____
_____
_____

Date_____

I am grateful for...

1. _____
2. _____
3. _____

What would make today great?

1. _____
2. _____
3. _____

Daily Affirmations. I am...

1. _____
2. _____
3. _____

Best part of my day today

_____
_____
_____

How could I have made today better?

_____
_____
_____

Date_____

I am grateful for...

1. _____
2. _____
3. _____

What would make today great?

1. _____
2. _____
3. _____

Daily Affirmations. I am...

1. _____
2. _____
3. _____

Best part of my day today

_____
_____
_____

How could I have made today better?

_____
_____
_____

Date_____

I AM GRATEFUL FOR…

1. _____
2. _____
3. _____

WHAT WOULD MAKE TODAY GREAT?

1. _____
2. _____
3. _____

DAILY AFFIRMATIONS. I AM…

1. _____
2. _____
3. _____

BEST PART OF MY DAY TODAY

_____
_____
_____

HOW COULD I HAVE MADE TODAY BETTER?

_____
_____
_____

DATE _____

I AM GRATEFUL FOR...

1. _____
2. _____
3. _____

WHAT WOULD MAKE TODAY GREAT ?

1. _____
2. _____
3. _____

DAILY AFFIRMATIONS. I AM...

1. _____
2. _____
3. _____

BEST PART OF MY DAY TODAY

_____
_____
_____

HOW COULD I HAVE MADE TODAY BETTER?

_____
_____
_____

Date_____

I am grateful for...

1. _____
2. _____
3. _____

What would make today great?

1. _____
2. _____
3. _____

Daily Affirmations. I am...

1. _____
2. _____
3. _____

Best part of my day today

_____
_____
_____

How could I have made today better?

_____
_____
_____

Date _____

I AM GRATEFUL FOR...

1. _____
2. _____
3. _____

WHAT WOULD MAKE TODAY GREAT ?

1. _____
2. _____
3. _____

DAILY AFFIRMATIONS. I AM...

1. _____
2. _____
3. _____

BEST PART OF MY DAY TODAY

_____
_____
_____

HOW COULD I HAVE MADE TODAY BETTER?

_____
_____
_____

Date_____

I AM GRATEFUL FOR...

1. _____
2. _____
3. _____

WHAT WOULD MAKE TODAY GREAT ?

1. _____
2. _____
3. _____

DAILY AFFIRMATIONS. I AM...

1. _____
2. _____
3. _____

BEST PART OF MY DAY TODAY

_____
_____
_____

HOW COULD I HAVE MADE TODAY BETTER?

_____
_____
_____

Date_____

I AM GRATEFUL FOR...

1. _____
2. _____
3. _____

WHAT WOULD MAKE TODAY GREAT ?

1. _____
2. _____
3. _____

DAILY AFFIRMATIONS. I AM...

1. _____
2. _____
3. _____

BEST PART OF MY DAY TODAY

_____
_____
_____

HOW COULD I HAVE MADE TODAY BETTER?

_____
_____
_____

Date_____

I am grateful for...

1. _____
2. _____
3. _____

What would make today great?

1. _____
2. _____
3. _____

Daily Affirmations. I am...

1. _____
2. _____
3. _____

Best part of my day today

_____
_____
_____

How could I have made today better?

_____
_____
_____

Date_____

I am grateful for...

1. _____
2. _____
3. _____

What would make today great?

1. _____
2. _____
3. _____

Daily Affirmations. I am...

1. _____
2. _____
3. _____

Best part of my day today

_____
_____
_____

How could I have made today better?

_____
_____
_____

Date_____

I am grateful for...

1. _____
2. _____
3. _____

What would make today great?

1. _____
2. _____
3. _____

Daily Affirmations. I am...

1. _____
2. _____
3. _____

Best part of my day today

_____
_____
_____

How could I have made today better?

_____
_____
_____

Date_____

I AM GRATEFUL FOR…

1. _____
2. _____
3. _____

WHAT WOULD MAKE TODAY GREAT ?

1. _____
2. _____
3. _____

DAILY AFFIRMATIONS. I AM…

1. _____
2. _____
3. _____

BEST PART OF MY DAY TODAY

_____
_____
_____

HOW COULD I HAVE MADE TODAY BETTER?

_____
_____
_____

Date_____

I am grateful for...

1. _____
2. _____
3. _____

What would make today great?

1. _____
2. _____
3. _____

Daily Affirmations. I am...

1. _____
2. _____
3. _____

Best part of my day today

_____
_____
_____

How could I have made today better?

_____
_____
_____

Date_____

I AM GRATEFUL FOR...

1. _____
2. _____
3. _____

WHAT WOULD MAKE TODAY GREAT?

1. _____
2. _____
3. _____

DAILY AFFIRMATIONS. I AM...

1. _____
2. _____
3. _____

BEST PART OF MY DAY TODAY

_____
_____
_____

HOW COULD I HAVE MADE TODAY BETTER?

_____
_____
_____

Date_____

I am grateful for...

1. _____
2. _____
3. _____

What would make today great?

1. _____
2. _____
3. _____

Daily Affirmations. I am...

1. _____
2. _____
3. _____

Best part of my day today

_____
_____
_____

How could I have made today better?

_____
_____
_____

Date_____

I AM GRATEFUL FOR...

1. _____
2. _____
3. _____

WHAT WOULD MAKE TODAY GREAT ?

1. _____
2. _____
3. _____

DAILY AFFIRMATIONS. I AM...

1. _____
2. _____
3. _____

BEST PART OF MY DAY TODAY

_____
_____
_____

HOW COULD I HAVE MADE TODAY BETTER?

_____
_____
_____

Date_____

I AM GRATEFUL FOR...

1. _____
2. _____
3. _____

WHAT WOULD MAKE TODAY GREAT ?

1. _____
2. _____
3. _____

DAILY AFFIRMATIONS. I AM...

1. _____
2. _____
3. _____

BEST PART OF MY DAY TODAY

_____
_____
_____

HOW COULD I HAVE MADE TODAY BETTER?

_____
_____
_____

Date_____

I am grateful for...

1. _____
2. _____
3. _____

What would make today great?

1. _____
2. _____
3. _____

Daily Affirmations. I am...

1. _____
2. _____
3. _____

Best part of my day today

_____
_____
_____

How could I have made today better?

_____
_____
_____

Date_____

I AM GRATEFUL FOR...

1. _____
2. _____
3. _____

WHAT WOULD MAKE TODAY GREAT ?

1. _____
2. _____
3. _____

DAILY AFFIRMATIONS. I AM...

1. _____
2. _____
3. _____

BEST PART OF MY DAY TODAY

_____
_____
_____

HOW COULD I HAVE MADE TODAY BETTER?

_____
_____
_____

Date_____

I AM GRATEFUL FOR...

1. _____
2. _____
3. _____

WHAT WOULD MAKE TODAY GREAT ?

1. _____
2. _____
3. _____

DAILY AFFIRMATIONS. I AM...

1. _____
2. _____
3. _____

BEST PART OF MY DAY TODAY

_____
_____
_____

HOW COULD I HAVE MADE TODAY BETTER?

_____
_____
_____

Date_____

I am grateful for...

1. _____
2. _____
3. _____

What would make today great?

1. _____
2. _____
3. _____

Daily Affirmations. I am...

1. _____
2. _____
3. _____

Best part of my day today

_____
_____
_____

How could I have made today better?

_____
_____
_____

Date_____

I am grateful for...

1. _____
2. _____
3. _____

What would make today great?

1. _____
2. _____
3. _____

Daily Affirmations. I am...

1. _____
2. _____
3. _____

Best part of my day today

_____
_____
_____

How could I have made today better?

_____
_____
_____

DATE_____

I AM GRATEFUL FOR...

1. _____
2. _____
3. _____

WHAT WOULD MAKE TODAY GREAT ?

1. _____
2. _____
3. _____

DAILY AFFIRMATIONS. I AM...

1. _____
2. _____
3. _____

BEST PART OF MY DAY TODAY

_____
_____
_____

HOW COULD I HAVE MADE TODAY BETTER?

_____
_____
_____

Date_____

I AM GRATEFUL FOR...

1. _____
2. _____
3. _____

WHAT WOULD MAKE TODAY GREAT ?

1. _____
2. _____
3. _____

DAILY AFFIRMATIONS. I AM...

1. _____
2. _____
3. _____

BEST PART OF MY DAY TODAY

_____
_____
_____

HOW COULD I HAVE MADE TODAY BETTER?

_____
_____
_____

Date_____

I AM GRATEFUL FOR...

1. _____
2. _____
3. _____

WHAT WOULD MAKE TODAY GREAT?

1. _____
2. _____
3. _____

DAILY AFFIRMATIONS. I AM...

1. _____
2. _____
3. _____

BEST PART OF MY DAY TODAY

_____
_____
_____

HOW COULD I HAVE MADE TODAY BETTER?

_____
_____
_____

Date_____

I am grateful for...

1. _____
2. _____
3. _____

What would make today great?

1. _____
2. _____
3. _____

Daily Affirmations. I am...

1. _____
2. _____
3. _____

Best part of my day today

_____
_____
_____

How could I have made today better?

_____
_____
_____

Date_____

I AM GRATEFUL FOR...

1. _____
2. _____
3. _____

WHAT WOULD MAKE TODAY GREAT ?

1. _____
2. _____
3. _____

DAILY AFFIRMATIONS. I AM...

1. _____
2. _____
3. _____

BEST PART OF MY DAY TODAY

_____
_____
_____

HOW COULD I HAVE MADE TODAY BETTER?

_____
_____
_____

DATE_____

I AM GRATEFUL FOR...

1. _____
2. _____
3. _____

WHAT WOULD MAKE TODAY GREAT ?

1. _____
2. _____
3. _____

DAILY AFFIRMATIONS. I AM...

1. _____
2. _____
3. _____

BEST PART OF MY DAY TODAY

_____
_____
_____

HOW COULD I HAVE MADE TODAY BETTER?

_____
_____
_____

Date_____

I AM GRATEFUL FOR...

1. _____
2. _____
3. _____

WHAT WOULD MAKE TODAY GREAT ?

1. _____
2. _____
3. _____

DAILY AFFIRMATIONS. I AM...

1. _____
2. _____
3. _____

BEST PART OF MY DAY TODAY

_____
_____
_____

HOW COULD I HAVE MADE TODAY BETTER?

_____
_____
_____

Date_____

I am grateful for...

1. _____
2. _____
3. _____

What would make today great?

1. _____
2. _____
3. _____

Daily Affirmations. I am...

1. _____
2. _____
3. _____

Best part of my day today

_____
_____
_____

How could I have made today better?

_____
_____
_____

DATE_____

I AM GRATEFUL FOR...

1. _____
2. _____
3. _____

WHAT WOULD MAKE TODAY GREAT ?

1. _____
2. _____
3. _____

DAILY AFFIRMATIONS. I AM...

1. _____
2. _____
3. _____

BEST PART OF MY DAY TODAY

_____
_____
_____

HOW COULD I HAVE MADE TODAY BETTER?

_____
_____
_____

Date_____

I am grateful for...

1. _____
2. _____
3. _____

What would make today great?

1. _____
2. _____
3. _____

Daily Affirmations. I am...

1. _____
2. _____
3. _____

Best part of my day today

_____
_____
_____

How could I have made today better?

_____
_____
_____

Date_____

I am grateful for...

1. _____
2. _____
3. _____

What would make today great?

1. _____
2. _____
3. _____

Daily Affirmations. I am...

1. _____
2. _____
3. _____

Best part of my day today

_____
_____
_____

How could I have made today better?

_____
_____
_____

Date_____

I am grateful for...

1. _____
2. _____
3. _____

What would make today great?

1. _____
2. _____
3. _____

Daily Affirmations. I am...

1. _____
2. _____
3. _____

Best part of my day today

_____
_____
_____

How could I have made today better?

_____
_____
_____

Date_____

I am grateful for...

1. _____
2. _____
3. _____

What would make today great ?

1. _____
2. _____
3. _____

Daily Affirmations. I am...

1. _____
2. _____
3. _____

Best part of my day today

_____
_____
_____

How could I have made today better?

_____
_____
_____

Date_____

I AM GRATEFUL FOR...

1. _____
2. _____
3. _____

WHAT WOULD MAKE TODAY GREAT ?

1. _____
2. _____
3. _____

DAILY AFFIRMATIONS. I AM...

1. _____
2. _____
3. _____

BEST PART OF MY DAY TODAY

_____
_____
_____

HOW COULD I HAVE MADE TODAY BETTER?

_____
_____
_____

Date_____

I am grateful for...

1. _____
2. _____
3. _____

What would make today great?

1. _____
2. _____
3. _____

Daily Affirmations. I am...

1. _____
2. _____
3. _____

Best part of my day today

_____
_____
_____

How could I have made today better?

_____
_____
_____

Date_____

I AM GRATEFUL FOR...

1. _____
2. _____
3. _____

WHAT WOULD MAKE TODAY GREAT ?

1. _____
2. _____
3. _____

DAILY AFFIRMATIONS. I AM...

1. _____
2. _____
3. _____

BEST PART OF MY DAY TODAY

_____
_____
_____

HOW COULD I HAVE MADE TODAY BETTER?

_____
_____
_____

Date_____

I am grateful for...

1. _____
2. _____
3. _____

What would make today great?

1. _____
2. _____
3. _____

Daily Affirmations. I am...

1. _____
2. _____
3. _____

Best part of my day today

_____
_____
_____

How could I have made today better?

_____
_____
_____

DATE_____

I AM GRATEFUL FOR...

1. _____
2. _____
3. _____

WHAT WOULD MAKE TODAY GREAT ?

1. _____
2. _____
3. _____

DAILY AFFIRMATIONS. I AM...

1. _____
2. _____
3. _____

BEST PART OF MY DAY TODAY

_____
_____
_____

HOW COULD I HAVE MADE TODAY BETTER?

_____
_____
_____

Date_____

I am grateful for...

1. _____
2. _____
3. _____

What would make today great?

1. _____
2. _____
3. _____

Daily Affirmations. I am...

1. _____
2. _____
3. _____

Best part of my day today

_____
_____
_____

How could I have made today better?

_____
_____
_____

Date_____

I am grateful for...

1. _____
2. _____
3. _____

What would make today great?

1. _____
2. _____
3. _____

Daily Affirmations. I am...

1. _____
2. _____
3. _____

Best part of my day today

_____
_____
_____

How could I have made today better?

_____
_____
_____

Date_____

I AM GRATEFUL FOR...

1. _____
2. _____
3. _____

WHAT WOULD MAKE TODAY GREAT ?

1. _____
2. _____
3. _____

DAILY AFFIRMATIONS. I AM...

1. _____
2. _____
3. _____

BEST PART OF MY DAY TODAY

_____
_____
_____

HOW COULD I HAVE MADE TODAY BETTER?

_____
_____
_____

Date_____

I am grateful for...

1. _____
2. _____
3. _____

What would make today great?

1. _____
2. _____
3. _____

Daily Affirmations. I am...

1. _____
2. _____
3. _____

Best part of my day today

_____
_____
_____

How could I have made today better?

_____
_____
_____

Date _____

I am grateful for...

1. _____
2. _____
3. _____

What would make today great?

1. _____
2. _____
3. _____

Daily Affirmations. I am...

1. _____
2. _____
3. _____

Best part of my day today

_____
_____
_____

How could I have made today better?

_____
_____
_____

Date_____

I am grateful for...

1. _____
2. _____
3. _____

What would make today great?

1. _____
2. _____
3. _____

Daily Affirmations. I am...

1. _____
2. _____
3. _____

Best part of my day today

_____
_____
_____

How could I have made today better?

_____
_____
_____

Date_____

I am grateful for...

1. _____
2. _____
3. _____

What would make today great?

1. _____
2. _____
3. _____

Daily Affirmations. I am...

1. _____
2. _____
3. _____

Best part of my day today

_____
_____
_____

How could I have made today better?

_____
_____

Date_____

I am grateful for...

1. _____
2. _____
3. _____

What would make today great?

1. _____
2. _____
3. _____

Daily Affirmations. I am...

1. _____
2. _____
3. _____

Best part of my day today

_____
_____
_____

How could I have made today better?

_____
_____
_____

Date_____

I am grateful for...

1. _____
2. _____
3. _____

What would make today great?

1. _____
2. _____
3. _____

Daily Affirmations. I am...

1. _____
2. _____
3. _____

Best part of my day today

_____
_____
_____

How could I have made today better?

_____
_____
_____

Date_____

I am grateful for...

1. _____
2. _____
3. _____

What would make today great?

1. _____
2. _____
3. _____

Daily Affirmations. I am...

1. _____
2. _____
3. _____

Best part of my day today

_____
_____
_____

How could I have made today better?

_____
_____
_____

Date_____

I AM GRATEFUL FOR...

1. _____
2. _____
3. _____

WHAT WOULD MAKE TODAY GREAT ?

1. _____
2. _____
3. _____

DAILY AFFIRMATIONS. I AM...

1. _____
2. _____
3. _____

BEST PART OF MY DAY TODAY

_____
_____
_____

HOW COULD I HAVE MADE TODAY BETTER?

_____
_____
_____

Date_____

I am grateful for...

1. _____
2. _____
3. _____

What would make today great?

1. _____
2. _____
3. _____

Daily Affirmations. I am...

1. _____
2. _____
3. _____

Best part of my day today

_____
_____
_____

How could I have made today better?

_____
_____
_____

Date_____

I AM GRATEFUL FOR...

1. _____
2. _____
3. _____

WHAT WOULD MAKE TODAY GREAT?

1. _____
2. _____
3. _____

DAILY AFFIRMATIONS. I AM...

1. _____
2. _____
3. _____

BEST PART OF MY DAY TODAY

_____
_____
_____

HOW COULD I HAVE MADE TODAY BETTER?

_____
_____
_____

Date_____

I AM GRATEFUL FOR...

1. _____
2. _____
3. _____

What would make today great?

1. _____
2. _____
3. _____

Daily Affirmations. I am...

1. _____
2. _____
3. _____

Best part of my day today

_____
_____
_____

How could I have made today better?

_____
_____
_____

Date_____

I am grateful for...

1. _____
2. _____
3. _____

What would make today great?

1. _____
2. _____
3. _____

Daily Affirmations. I am...

1. _____
2. _____
3. _____

Best part of my day today

_____
_____
_____

How could I have made today better?

_____
_____
_____

DATE_____

I AM GRATEFUL FOR...

1. _____
2. _____
3. _____

WHAT WOULD MAKE TODAY GREAT ?

1. _____
2. _____
3. _____

DAILY AFFIRMATIONS. I AM...

1. _____
2. _____
3. _____

BEST PART OF MY DAY TODAY

_____
_____
_____

HOW COULD I HAVE MADE TODAY BETTER?

_____
_____
_____

Date_____

I am grateful for...

1. _____
2. _____
3. _____

What would make today great?

1. _____
2. _____
3. _____

Daily Affirmations. I am...

1. _____
2. _____
3. _____

Best part of my day today

_____
_____
_____

How could I have made today better?

_____
_____
_____

Date_____

I am grateful for...

1. _____
2. _____
3. _____

What would make today great?

1. _____
2. _____
3. _____

Daily Affirmations. I am...

1. _____
2. _____
3. _____

Best part of my day today

_____
_____
_____

How could I have made today better?

_____
_____
_____

Date_____

I am grateful for...

1. _____
2. _____
3. _____

What would make today great?

1. _____
2. _____
3. _____

Daily Affirmations. I am...

1. _____
2. _____
3. _____

Best part of my day today

_____
_____
_____

How could I have made today better?

_____
_____
_____

Date_____

I am grateful for...

1. _____
2. _____
3. _____

What would make today great?

1. _____
2. _____
3. _____

Daily Affirmations. I am...

1. _____
2. _____
3. _____

Best part of my day today

_____
_____
_____

How could I have made today better?

_____
_____
_____

Date_____

I am grateful for...

1. _____
2. _____
3. _____

What would make today great?

1. _____
2. _____
3. _____

Daily Affirmations. I am...

1. _____
2. _____
3. _____

Best part of my day today

_____
_____
_____

How could I have made today better?

_____
_____
_____

Date_____

I am grateful for...

1. _____
2. _____
3. _____

What would make today great?

1. _____
2. _____
3. _____

Daily Affirmations. I am...

1. _____
2. _____
3. _____

Best part of my day today

_____
_____
_____

How could I have made today better?

_____
_____
_____

Date_____

I am grateful for...

1. _____
2. _____
3. _____

What would make today great?

1. _____
2. _____
3. _____

Daily Affirmations. I am...

1. _____
2. _____
3. _____

Best part of my day today

_____
_____
_____

How could I have made today better?

_____
_____
_____

Date_____

I AM GRATEFUL FOR...

1. _____
2. _____
3. _____

WHAT WOULD MAKE TODAY GREAT ?

1. _____
2. _____
3. _____

DAILY AFFIRMATIONS. I AM...

1. _____
2. _____
3. _____

BEST PART OF MY DAY TODAY

_____
_____
_____

HOW COULD I HAVE MADE TODAY BETTER?

_____
_____
_____

Date_____

I AM GRATEFUL FOR...

1. _____
2. _____
3. _____

WHAT WOULD MAKE TODAY GREAT ?

1. _____
2. _____
3. _____

DAILY AFFIRMATIONS. I AM...

1. _____
2. _____
3. _____

BEST PART OF MY DAY TODAY

_____
_____
_____

HOW COULD I HAVE MADE TODAY BETTER?

_____
_____
_____

Date_____

I AM GRATEFUL FOR...

1. _____
2. _____
3. _____

WHAT WOULD MAKE TODAY GREAT ?

1. _____
2. _____
3. _____

DAILY AFFIRMATIONS. I AM...

1. _____
2. _____
3. _____

BEST PART OF MY DAY TODAY

_____
_____
_____

HOW COULD I HAVE MADE TODAY BETTER?

_____
_____
_____

DATE_____

I AM GRATEFUL FOR...

1. _____
2. _____
3. _____

WHAT WOULD MAKE TODAY GREAT?

1. _____
2. _____
3. _____

DAILY AFFIRMATIONS. I AM...

1. _____
2. _____
3. _____

BEST PART OF MY DAY TODAY

_____
_____
_____

HOW COULD I HAVE MADE TODAY BETTER?

_____
_____
_____

Date_____

I am grateful for...

1. _____
2. _____
3. _____

What would make today great?

1. _____
2. _____
3. _____

Daily Affirmations. I am...

1. _____
2. _____
3. _____

Best part of my day today

_____
_____
_____

How could I have made today better?

_____
_____
_____

Date_____

I AM GRATEFUL FOR…

1. _____
2. _____
3. _____

WHAT WOULD MAKE TODAY GREAT ?

1. _____
2. _____
3. _____

DAILY AFFIRMATIONS. I AM…

1. _____
2. _____
3. _____

BEST PART OF MY DAY TODAY

_____
_____
_____

HOW COULD I HAVE MADE TODAY BETTER?

_____
_____
_____

Date_____

I am grateful for...

1. _____
2. _____
3. _____

What would make today great?

1. _____
2. _____
3. _____

Daily Affirmations. I am...

1. _____
2. _____
3. _____

Best part of my day today

_____
_____
_____

How could I have made today better?

_____
_____
_____

Date_____

I am grateful for...

1. _____
2. _____
3. _____

What would make today great?

1. _____
2. _____
3. _____

Daily Affirmations. I am...

1. _____
2. _____
3. _____

Best part of my day today

_____
_____
_____

How could I have made today better?

_____
_____
_____

Date_____

I AM GRATEFUL FOR...

1. _____
2. _____
3. _____

WHAT WOULD MAKE TODAY GREAT?

1. _____
2. _____
3. _____

DAILY AFFIRMATIONS. I AM...

1. _____
2. _____
3. _____

BEST PART OF MY DAY TODAY

_____
_____
_____

HOW COULD I HAVE MADE TODAY BETTER?

_____
_____
_____

Date_____

I AM GRATEFUL FOR...

1. _____
2. _____
3. _____

WHAT WOULD MAKE TODAY GREAT?

1. _____
2. _____
3. _____

DAILY AFFIRMATIONS. I AM...

1. _____
2. _____
3. _____

BEST PART OF MY DAY TODAY

_____
_____
_____

HOW COULD I HAVE MADE TODAY BETTER?

_____
_____
_____

Date_____

I AM GRATEFUL FOR…

1. _____
2. _____
3. _____

WHAT WOULD MAKE TODAY GREAT ?

1. _____
2. _____
3. _____

DAILY AFFIRMATIONS. I AM…

1. _____
2. _____
3. _____

BEST PART OF MY DAY TODAY

_____
_____
_____

HOW COULD I HAVE MADE TODAY BETTER?

_____
_____
_____

DATE_____

I AM GRATEFUL FOR...

1. _____
2. _____
3. _____

WHAT WOULD MAKE TODAY GREAT?

1. _____
2. _____
3. _____

DAILY AFFIRMATIONS. I AM...

1. _____
2. _____
3. _____

BEST PART OF MY DAY TODAY

_____
_____
_____

HOW COULD I HAVE MADE TODAY BETTER?

_____
_____
_____

Date_____

I am grateful for...

1. _____
2. _____
3. _____

What would make today great?

1. _____
2. _____
3. _____

Daily Affirmations. I am...

1. _____
2. _____
3. _____

Best part of my day today

_____
_____
_____

How could I have made today better?

_____
_____
_____

Date_____

I AM GRATEFUL FOR...

1. _____
2. _____
3. _____

WHAT WOULD MAKE TODAY GREAT ?

1. _____
2. _____
3. _____

DAILY AFFIRMATIONS. I AM...

1. _____
2. _____
3. _____

BEST PART OF MY DAY TODAY

_____
_____
_____

HOW COULD I HAVE MADE TODAY BETTER?

_____
_____
_____

Date_____

I am grateful for...

1. _____
2. _____
3. _____

What would make today great?

1. _____
2. _____
3. _____

Daily Affirmations. I am...

1. _____
2. _____
3. _____

Best part of my day today

_____
_____
_____

How could I have made today better?

_____
_____
_____

Date_____

I am grateful for...

1. _____
2. _____
3. _____

What would make today great?

1. _____
2. _____
3. _____

Daily Affirmations. I am...

1. _____
2. _____
3. _____

Best part of my day today

_____
_____
_____

How could I have made today better?

_____
_____
_____

Date_____

I am grateful for...

1. _____
2. _____
3. _____

What would make today great?

1. _____
2. _____
3. _____

Daily Affirmations. I am...

1. _____
2. _____
3. _____

Best part of my day today

_____
_____
_____

How could I have made today better?

_____
_____
_____

Date_____

I AM GRATEFUL FOR...

1. _____
2. _____
3. _____

WHAT WOULD MAKE TODAY GREAT ?

1. _____
2. _____
3. _____

DAILY AFFIRMATIONS. I AM...

1. _____
2. _____
3. _____

BEST PART OF MY DAY TODAY

_____
_____
_____

HOW COULD I HAVE MADE TODAY BETTER?

_____
_____
_____

Date_____

I AM GRATEFUL FOR...

1. _____
2. _____
3. _____

WHAT WOULD MAKE TODAY GREAT ?

1. _____
2. _____
3. _____

DAILY AFFIRMATIONS. I AM...

1. _____
2. _____
3. _____

BEST PART OF MY DAY TODAY

_____
_____
_____

HOW COULD I HAVE MADE TODAY BETTER?

_____
_____
_____

Date_____

I am grateful for…

1. _____
2. _____
3. _____

What would make today great?

1. _____
2. _____
3. _____

Daily Affirmations. I am…

1. _____
2. _____
3. _____

Best part of my day today

_____
_____
_____

How could I have made today better?

_____
_____
_____

Date_____

I am grateful for...

1. _____
2. _____
3. _____

What would make today great?

1. _____
2. _____
3. _____

Daily Affirmations. I am...

1. _____
2. _____
3. _____

Best part of my day today

_____
_____
_____

How could I have made today better?

_____
_____
_____

Date_____

I am grateful for...

1. _____
2. _____
3. _____

What would make today great?

1. _____
2. _____
3. _____

Daily Affirmations. I am...

1. _____
2. _____
3. _____

Best part of my day today

_____
_____
_____

How could I have made today better?

_____
_____
_____

Date_____

I am grateful for...

1. _____
2. _____
3. _____

What would make today great?

1. _____
2. _____
3. _____

Daily Affirmations. I am...

1. _____
2. _____
3. _____

Best part of my day today

_____
_____
_____

How could I have made today better?

_____
_____
_____

Date_____

I am grateful for...

1. _____
2. _____
3. _____

What would make today great?

1. _____
2. _____
3. _____

Daily Affirmations. I am...

1. _____
2. _____
3. _____

Best part of my day today

_____
_____
_____

How could I have made today better?

_____
_____
_____

Made in United States
North Haven, CT
05 June 2023